Scary States (of Mind)

Horror in Virginia

by Thomas Persano

Consultant: Debbie Felton
Professor of Classics
University of Massachusetts
Amherst, Massachusetts

Bearport Publishing
Minneapolis, Minnesota

Credits

Cover, © Kim Jones, © Doug Hendricks/Shutterstock, © avevizavi_com/Shutterstock, © Lopolo/Shutterstock, and © cosma/Shutterstock; 3, © Katelyn N. Thomas/Shutterstock; 4-5, © Kim Jones, © vladimir salman/Shutterstock, © Kathy Clark/Shutterstock, and © Breck P. Kent/Shutterstock; 6, © TaraPatta/Shutterstock; 7, © William Silver/Shutterstock; 7TL, © Surfsci1117/Wikimedia Commons/Creative Commons; 7TR, © Virginia Historical Society/Wikimedia Commons/Public Domain; 8-9, © Elisanth/Shutterstock; 9, © Andrey_Popov/Shutterstock; 10, Wikimedia/Public Domain; 11, © Jon Bilous/Shutterstock; 12, © Number 86/Shutterstock; 13, © Fopseh/Wikimedia Commons/Creative Commons; 14, © Viktoriia Bondarenko/Shutterstock; 15, Kurz & Allison/Wikimedia Commons/Creative Commons; 16-17, © Pat & Chuck Blackley/Alamy and © Everett Historical/Shutterstock; 18, © Dario Racane/Shutterstock; 19, © Petra holden/Wikimedia Commons; 20T, © David Evison/Shutterstock; 20B, © Donna Beeler/Shutterstock; 21, © Dee-n/Shutterstock © Ljupco Smokovski/Shutterstock; 23, © Ricky Of The World/Shutterstock; and 24, © Vera Petruk/Shutterstock.

President: Jen Jenson
Director of Product Development: Spencer Brinker
Editor: Allison Juda
Designer: Micah Edel
Cover: Kim Jones

Library of Congress Cataloging-in-Publication Data

Names: Persano, Thomas, author.
Title: Horror in Virginia / by Thomas Persano.
Description: Minneapolis : Bearport Publishing Company, [2021] | Series: Scary states (of mind) | Includes bibliographical references and index.
Identifiers: LCCN 2020000515 (print) | LCCN 2020000516 (ebook) | ISBN 9781647470791 (library binding) | ISBN 9781647470890 (ebook)
Subjects: LCSH: Haunted places—Virginia—Juvenile literature. | Ghosts—Virginia—Juvenile literature. | Virginia—Miscellanea—Juvenile literature.
Classification: LCC BF1472.U6 P425 2021 (print) | LCC BF1472.U6 (ebook) | DDC 133.109755—dc23
LC record available at https://lccn.loc.gov/2020000515
LC ebook record available at https://lccn.loc.gov/2020000516

For more information, write to Bearport Publishing, 5357 Penn Avenue South, Minneapolis, MN 55419. Printed in the United States of America.

CONTENTS

Horror in Virginia

Virginia is a state with a rich history. But have the ghosts of the past decided to stay there forever? **Cursed** spirits wander its streets. It's best to keep a look out—you may come face-to-face with a dark shadow!

Get ready to read four **eerie** stories about Virginia. Turn the page . . . if you dare.

Cursed Souls

Peyton Randolph House, Colonial Williamsburg

Peyton and Betty Randolph were very **cruel** to their **enslaved** workers. Betty stole a baby from an enslaved woman named Eve and gave it away. In response, Eve cursed the Randolphs and their house.

Since then, shadowy figures have appeared in the windows when the house should be empty. Mirrors have mysteriously shattered. A **phantom** woman has been heard singing a gloomy song.

Betty Randolph

Peyton Randolph

Peyton Randolph House

The Peyton Randolph House is now a museum. One night, a security guard heard strange sounds in the basement. After finding no one there, he turned to leave. Suddenly, something grabbed his ankles and tried to pull him down. He escaped but was shaken by the event. Is the Peyton Randolph House still under Eve's curse?

Over the years, many people have tragically died in the house. Some deaths were accidents, but others were murders!

Spirit School

Swannanoa Palace, Afton

James and Sallie May Dooley built Swannanoa Palace in 1912 deep in the Blue Ridge Mountains. After their deaths, the home was **abandoned** until an artist named Walter Russell started an unusual school there.

The students learned about the **supernatural** and discussed alien life. They also tried to make contact with spirits from another world.

James Dooley

Swannanoa Palace

The strange school closed, but rumors spread that the ghost of Sallie May could be seen drifting through the palace. Spirits of old workers have been heard whispering in the hallways. Did the students open a doorway to the spirit world that let Swannanoa Palace's former residents return home?

A group of **investigators** recorded strange sounds at the palace that they said were voices of the dead.

Inside Swannanoa Palace

FIELD OF NIGHTMARES

Cold Harbor Battlefield, Mechanicsville

The bloody Battle of Cold Harbor was fought during the Civil War (1861–1865). It was so violent that visitors to the battlefield can sometimes still hear the gunfire, battle cries, moans, and running horses. Some nights, the field suddenly becomes covered in an eerie fog that **vanishes** just as quickly as it settles in.

Battle of Cold Harbor

One visitor may even know what it felt like to be in the battle. He was standing in the middle of a field in Mechanicsville when he felt a terrible pain on the side of his head.

The visitor had been standing on the spot where a **colonel** had been shot in the head during the fight.

In only 12 days of fighting, more than 2,000 soldiers died during the Battle of Cold Harbor.

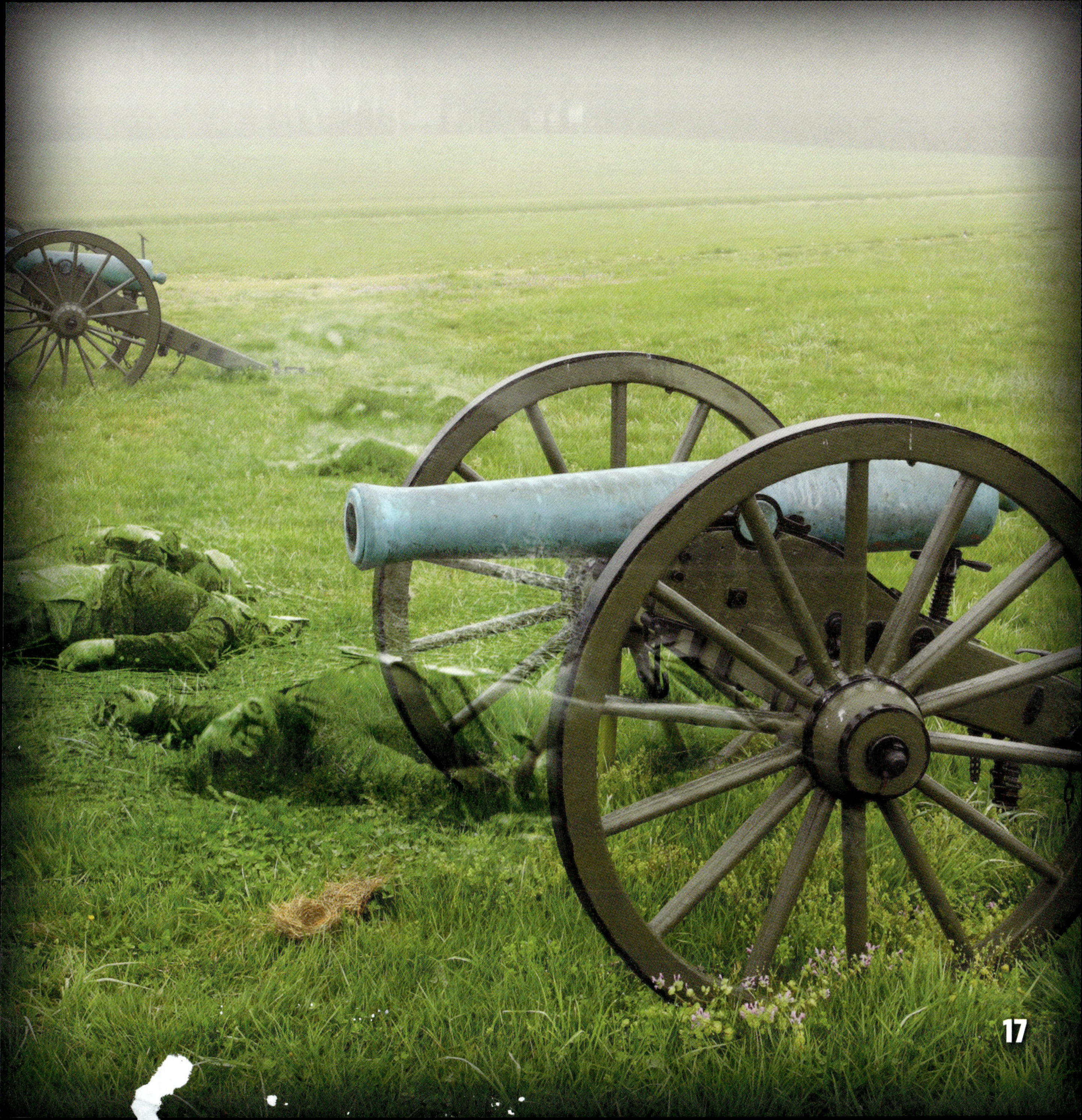

A Friendly Ghost

Boxwood Inn Bed & Breakfast, Newport News

Some hauntings are less scary than others. Boxwood Inn is home to a friendly and hardworking ghost.

Nannie Cooke Curtis and her husband, Simon, built their house in 1897. They lived upstairs, and Nannie worked in the general store on the first floor. The house has since become the Boxwood Inn, where strange things happen to visitors.

Boxwood Inn Bed & Breakfast

Sometimes the ghost of Nannie wakes guests with loud knocking at six in the morning. This is when she used to start work at the store.

Some guests have been given small gifts. One woman broke her nail, and a nail file suddenly appeared so she could fix it. Is Nannie still taking care of her customers?

Inn guests have also reported seeing a ghostly old man with a cane walking around.

Spooky Spots in Virginia

Cold Harbor Battlefield
Explore the battlefield where thousands of soldiers died.

Peyton Randolph House
Experience the sad history of this historic building.

Swannanoa Palace
Learn about the supernatural at this haunted home.

Boxwood Inn Bed & Breakfast
Run into a helpful ghost when you stay at this haunted inn.

GLOSSARY

abandoned (uh-BAN-duhnd) empty or no longer used

colonel (KUR-nuhl) a military officer of high rank

cruel (KROO-uhl) causing or helping to cause suffering

cursed (KURST) bringing unhappiness or bad luck

eerie (IHR-ee) mysterious or strange

enslaved (en-SLAVED) made to be a person who is owned by others and who is forced to do hard work without pay

investigators (in-VESS-ti-ga-tors) people who try to solve mysteries using proof and evidence

phantom (FAN-tuhm) a ghost

supernatural (*soo*-pur-NACH-ur-uhl) something ghostly or unusual that can't be easily explained

vanishes (VA-nih-shiz) disappears

INDEX

READ MORE

Camisa, Kathryn. *Horror Hotels (Tiptoe Into Scary Places).* New York: Bearport (2017).

Rudolph, Jessica. *Ghost Houses (Tiptoe Into Scary Places).* New York: Bearport (2017).

LEARN MORE ONLINE

1. Go to **www.factsurfer.com**
2. Enter "**Horror in Virginia**" into the search box.
3. Click on the cover of this book to see a list of websites.

ABOUT THE AUTHOR

Thomas Persano lives in New York City. He has never seen a ghost in his life, but he wouldn't mind meeting a friendly one someday.